My Life in Squares

My Life in Squares
Kristin Dimitrova

Published 2010 by
Smokestack Books
PO Box 408, Middlesbrough TS5 6WA
e-mail : info@smokestack-books.co.uk
www.smokestack-books.co.uk

My Life in Squares
Kristin Dmitrova
Copyright 2010, Kristin Dmitrova, all rights reserved
Translated by Kristin Dimitrova and Vladimir Trendafilov
Cover photo: Jean-Marc Caracci, Homo Urbanus Europeanus –
Sofia no6
Author photo: Radomira Chipeva

Printed by
EPW Print & Design Ltd

ISBN 978-0-9560341-7-5
Smokestack Books gratefully
acknowledges the support of
Arts Council England

LOTTERY FUNDED

Smokestack Books is
represented by Inpress Ltd
www.inpressbooks.co.uk

Contents

- 9   My Life in Squares
- 10   After Babylon
- 11   Opportunities
- 12   The Sanatorium of Other People's Deaths
- 13   Reading for the Road
- 14   What is there at My Disposal
- 15   Spring Checking of the Mail
- 16   The Three Lady Beggars at the Book Premiere
- 17   The Inspectors' Lodge
- 18   Daylight
- 19   And Expanses to Run
- 20   The Planet of the Pensioners
- 21   Solve et Coagula
- 22   The Groove
- 23   A Day Out on Vitosha Mountain
- 24   A Dance with the Creator
- 25   The Coming One
- 26   The Morning of the Cardplayer
- 27   The Monument
- 28   The Architectress
- 29   Conversations with the Undying
- 30   About the Origin of Species
- 31   In the Frame
- 32   On the Eve of the Big and the Small Things
- 33   The Good People
- 34   At the Site of the Excavations
- 35   A Lake Accident
- 36   The Strong Skins of Memory
- 37   365 Days, One of Them Circled
- 38   The Circle
- 39   Our Friends Come Back to Open Our Eyes
- 40   Visiting Hours
- 41   My Grandmother and I
- 42   Cat Exhibition
- 43   Omens
- 44   A Plan

45 Linda
46 The Pigeon
47 Faith
48 So We Shall Fly Through Space
49 Closed Figures
50 A Summit Meeting
51 Parting
52 The Wedding of Life, Sleep and Death
53 Ivanka Wants to Kill Her Daughter
54 The Fear
55 The Harbour
57 Free Fall
58 Passing by the City of Sort
59 The Truth Will Make You Free
60 The Conversationalist
61 The Winner
62 The Trace
63 Advantage
64 St. Valentine is a Martyr of Ancient Rome
65 Eva
66 Asen
67 Feelings
68 The Colonel's Widow
69 The Bald Boy
70 Reconstruing the Scene
71 A Few Extra Chromosomes
72 Tibet
73 Sometimes it is Not Important Who Sings
74 The Garden of Exquisite Silence
75 In the Third Quarter
76 And a Key is no Longer Necessary
77 A Premonition of a Dream
78 The Refuge
79 At the End of the Summer
80 The Breeder
81 An Epic
82 The Awakening
83 The Game

My Life in Squares

Like a chess-player who plays with
both the white and the black pieces,
I have been attacking myself
for a long while.
At each turn of the chessboard

I defend myself against enemy bishops.
The knight's horses snort, stamping their feet,
and when they jump, their hoofs
pierce through chest bones.
The queen is laughing at me.

Today the white one.
Tomorrow the black one.
I hear her while I think
over my next move.
Some people end

this kind of game
with an inevitable victory.
I get upset,
kick down the chessboard
and storm out of the room.

Then I ponder over my loss and see
that it was so damn unfair.

After Babylon

And so without laboratories,
and so without conservatories,
and so without observatories,

the small town sighs in the afternoon;
pears drop down through people's dreams
and the town clock is struck dumb at

ten to five like a calf gaping
at the men in bloodstained aprons.
The mosque was once the tallest building here,

later the church gained advantage in
walling off the air
for higher purposes.

But there is no proud
tower and the languages
are already divided

more or less.
Two girls are coming from the baker's,
picking at the bread crust.

And then at night - the glow of TV screens,
curtains to keep out the darkness
and two-story plans for the future.

The stars, gone feral in packs,
creep silently down,
unaccounted for.

Opportunities

Where should I go
what should I do
where should I go
what should I do
so stuck in my skin
I grope for a zipper
and out of the open
jagged slit
I will slip out,
all muscles.
My skin will keep on saying
good morning while going to work
for another couple of years at least.

The Sanatorium of Other People's Deaths

The ailing house towers over
the edge of all minutes and the stars
can be seen below.

In the afternoon the rehab room is lit up,
and at night only a few windows
where insomnia chases the day's news.

The newspapers are letters
from yesterday's world, which is no more,
and you just can't know what

really happened.
The air is clear and willingly enters
the lame lungs.

There, oh there.
There people with transplanted odds and bits
walk about and answer each question with

'by and by.' They wrap their dressing-gowns
around their bodies, strange to the world,
each one riveted onto a heart that tells

a stranger's
horrible story.

Reading for the Road

At his hotel destination he clutched
a glowing glass of cognac among unfamiliar hills
for the time being. The receptionist girl
sucked him in through her thick glasses
and handed him a notepad. Sir,
there is a message for you
from your wife.
Thank you, I haven't got a wife,
but when I find one,
I'll read it.

What is There at My Disposal

The weed in the pot gesticulates
like the first and only guest
at a birthday party. The other seeds
never showed up.
Silently they refused to take part
in the fair of transformations -
thesis, antithesis, synthesis;
even their theses remained hidden.
Yesterday I poked the soil around;
they were all gone.
I just found two or three round bodies
clenching their teeth in stiff tenacity,
oval
memories of an opportunity.

The weed signals me to shut up,
it looks hurt.

I don't know its name, I don't like it.
It appeared in place of the
unfulfilled flowers.
I water it.

Spring Checking of the Mail

This year once again
I searched and searched in the new grass,
but maybe this is the desirable thing,
the regular thing –

the four leaf clover
is a freak, isn't it?

The Three Lady Beggars at the Book Premiere

We all know each other, more or less.
>We listen to the reading author
>with attention.

No one knows the three
>grey old women
>in the audience.

When we hear the long awaited 'help yourselves, please'
>the three grey ladies
>hurry to the buffet.

We turn our heads away from them.
>Their rotten smell reminds us
>of our exit-fee.

They advance without noticing us.
>Beggars regard the others not as people
>but as territory.

The three have no place among us.

>We all talk of literature,
>we will not fill our stomachs with the cheese rolls
>and we step back squeamishly
>from the reeking gash into a world
>that gapes at our cheese rolls,
>and has neither read, nor heard of literature.

We search for meaning. We came here
>to treat people to books;
>part of the meaning came –

to claim our cheese rolls.

The Inspectors' Lodge

In the Ministry of Leaves I am
        a middle employee –
the ants are below me, two or three stars
are above me, each one with a portfolio. We count the veins,
measure the gear wheels of the planets,
keep a watchful eye open but outwardly we look
like anyone else who has never ever
        finished anything.
This gives us away.

Daylight

Like an ant that hauls a crumb
but has forgotten where the ant-hill is,
she stares at details,

then cleans the sink very carefully.
These things that happen in films,
who invents them?

So now, between two men –
the first one history and the other
still in the coffee-grounds –

she seeks protection for herself
when she doesn't seek protection
from herself. As for the telephone,

sometimes it rings, sometimes it babbles,
the third time she broke it.
What a boundless abyss of time past

and future, Marcus Aurelius,
I agree. And in the middle, a button
that says 'don't touch'.

And Expanses to Run

Like a glass of good water left
in the sun for too long,
poetry – what a feast,
what a glory, what a necessity –
who are we to group words
in unnatural poses?
The poet's legs stick
helplessly towards the sky,
trying to walk.

The Planet of the Pensioners

Here, instead of a sun, two moons shine.
No chimneys smoke – corners must be cut.
The planet of the pensioners
has sheltered them in thin houses.

The small jars on the window sill hold:

a happy seaside summer, little fishes
dash over the reclining lovers,

two black locks – can you believe it,

the last meeting with the granddaughter
for the month.

These are taken only evenings, with a teaspoon,
for they might harm the heart.

Portraits hang above the shelf,
their faces soaked into the paper.
Gone over to the other side,
they wait.

After 9 the white mound of the quilt
portends a peaceful rest.

Before dawn a discolored colonel
jumps his horse out of the frame
of a yellowish photo and invites
the old woman to dance.

'No, it's too early,' she pushes him away
and tucks herself up, hoping for tomorrow.

Solve et Coagula

Your glasses watch me over the table
while your gloves rub hands in the corner.
Two socks peek timidly
from under the couch and
your sweater bristles
on the back of the armchair,
        sleeve on the heart.
Only you are out of here,
supposedly, but have invaded the world
with your parts
like Osiris who waits
to be pieced together,
but does not really want to.

The Groove

You think
There's a lake beyond this wood,
and you may be right but
it's not for you.
Once you start for the lake
and walk through the wood, the world
will curve upwards
steeper and steeper
until you find yourself climbing vertically.
Above your head the lake
will trace transparent circles

> by the spread tablecloth of an unknown family.
> The wife pours coffee from a thermos,
> the husband skips pebbles across the water
> for the youngest son's delight.
> She stares at you.

You don't know them.
You'll never meet them again.
Down there waits the track
your feet will walk on
their fastest.
The rest is an etching.

A Day Out on Mt Vitosha

Cranks in anoraks,
old men with small curved knives
for picking penny buns.
And naughty mountain regulars
stretching out their stares
for a handshake.
Women in threes
discussing ardently some broken love-affair.
Through the holes among the new leaves
the sky has penetrated to the ferns.
Students with ecologically clean looks
search for a civilized path
to make it up to nature.
The air smells of sweating garlic sausage,
eggshells and thyme
and thyme
and thyme
when all steps die away.
The forest is a solace and a dream,
95% unfulfilled.

A Dance with the Creator

The paper doll you cut
along the outlines of your body,
fluttered its flat fingers when
you danced together in jest –
she accidentally stirred by your life,
you with a minute cut-out of
your profile.

The Coming One

No, he was neither
fat nor skinny,
neither tall nor short,

neither good nor evil,
only neutral, like a geometric point –
massless, but how it punctures the sheet.

He had white, shiny bones and –
wrapped in a mantle of a missing
colour – he carried, in a fifteenth-century fashion,

a scythe.
I was walking back from the store while he
was probably on his way there, for how

else would I meet him, and
he stood in my way.
I asked him who he was.

I will come twice, he answered,
once at 7, and then once again.
At 7am I woke up.

The Morning of the Cardplayer

Good-morning, eyes.
Give a smile.

Old ladies sold you roots in your dream,
and the day doesn't look happier.

Then what makes the pigeon in the back yard
sing, or maybe it tries

to say something completely different?
Time isn't friendly

because it hides its graceful mechanics, but
there are enough folds in its hide

where one can find refuge.
I make coffee. Lay the table.

Divide my small change
into before and now, just to make sure

in what currency I'll pay today.
I will communicate with the reflections on the signs.

They will communicate with the reflections of my face.
And everything will be real as much

as it can.
In the distance I hear a rearranging of

cogwheels. A card will come out
of the slot. It is this card

I live for.

The Monument

The monument of pale truths
brings me to tears.
Raising a concrete forehead
against the meteorites
it is obviously unaware
that its foundation crumbles.
Here, my soft feet too
add their violence.
B from DRUZHBA has tilted down
in a suicidal endeavour.
Inside, like in every true pyramid,
there are entrances,
tunnels
shafts,
welded iron doors.
Water is dripping somewhere.
And it is quiet
and white
as if you have entered
the long decayed skull of a madman.
Somebody had written on the wall
in big blue letters
'Eric Clapton is no God'.
Small wonder.

The Architectress

The architectress carries blueprints.
Only the slab is poured. The walls
are transparent and rise from everywhere
strictly according to layout.
The architectress has spread the blueprints
on the nonexistent windowsill,
leafs through them for mistakes,
then leans and looks through a window
no less transparent.
The architectress (technically)
doesn't exist.
Which makes the house good enough

and practically finished.

Conversations with the Undying

Above the city cherubs
with puffed-up cheeks pile up,
the last sun rays shooting down
through their downy wings.

The sunset is a second-hand sunrise.

I have just donated blood
and under my second-hand overcoat
I hide a very proud body.
Its blood liquids, corpuscles
and so-and-sos
wait in a jar
to pull somebody
back to life.

Unknowingly, I'll whisper
wake up, wake up.
My blood cells, just a little used,
will bring you back
by the hand.

Perhaps I myself am second-hand.
I have come back many times and the world is
an easy fit for me, like a loose overcoat.

Cherubs, winged buttocks
with eternal babyfaces,
I am trying to tell you about life.

No way you can get it.

About the Origin of Species

From the extraterrestrial parasites,
who suck people dry from the inside
and rule the world by
the levers of their hands,
through the clones with souls
to the bat-human hybrid,

I follow the news about the Martians,
waiting for an invasion.
'Afraid they might leave you
behind, huh?' my mother throws in.

Shut up, Mum, I don't expect
even you to know anything.

They all drug them unconscious.

In the Frame

I am reordering the pictures.
The one in the sea-water frame
comes to the fore.
The one in which we enclosed
      smoke of dry leaves
goes to the back room.
I get very excited sometimes and
run out of paints.
They flow down into a forest
      with a lake,
too lazy to depict anything more
than a wood bench.
I like to go there.
I lie in the sun with all my
      one-time cats
and imagine how I wait for you
expecting to see other friends as well.
Thus I fade out in
      other people's pictures,
as my own one becomes brighter
and I feel finished.

On the Eve of the Big and the Small Things

She had two dots tattooed
on each side of her mouth.
She sat facing backwards
in the bus and could see only
the past of our journey which
anyway went in a circle.

'But my boy wouldn't grow,' she said
to the woman across from her
'his head, his legs remained
just the same and the doctors
saw this, but you don't have to be
a doctor at all to...'

The dots by her mouth
gathered and pulled apart, and
dropped down in her mid-sentences.
The world was preparing for war
while she was coming back from her own one,
a veteran, tattooed

with her ugly amulets.
The sky was curdled
like a frightened mind
or a red soup which many people stir
but still it clots.

The Good People

He is a very good person.
The trouble is that good people
are too many and they
keep stepping on each other's toes,
and during the scuffle
the world grows hotter,
so please now don't be cross with me
though I can see you folding your eyebrows
from the height of your goodness.

At the Site of the Excavations

The sinking of earth's crust raises questions
and buries the answers.
In your house, divided in two,
half of the sitting room connects with
                          the upper floor bedroom,
the attic meets the bathroom
and the kitchen had slipped down
as far as the entrance hall.

Something lost its door and
the torn staircase now ends into the ground.
Deep down, they went to rest –
the hugged out teddy bear,
a few school notebooks
with big squares,
a letter to a friend in block capitals
and instruments
                      you can find in any other cellar.

    What instruments?

Instruments of the kind
you have probably seen, but never knew
what they were used for.
Such kind of instruments.

(what instruments)

The connections are cut.
No door leads there now,
no way how to get down,
you will never find out
                  what remained inside,
            why your father gets his dates wrong
              where your mother's scissors disappeared.

Let it rest.
Let it rest and, like all of us,
spend the night on the roof.

A Lake Accident

Now I remember
that we played
but to my mind
I didn't know them.
They came from other
neighbourhoods
in their stained
T-shirts and worn-
Out traners
They just dropped by.
We almost played.
I almost left the others.

> *'Come away, o come away,'*
> *the children shouted sore,*
> *waving their hands, while I*
> *stood looking from the door.*

They went to swim,
they seemed to want it.
Then seemed to swim away.
So I remained while they
just vanished.

Now I can almost see them
as they vanish over
the livid waters of the lake,
and smile in other
people's calendars.

> *'Come away, o come away,'*
> *the children shouted so,*
> *waving their hands above the water,*
> *as I remained below.*

The Strong Skins of Memory

'Your skin is as smooth as
a Man United fan's, my love,'
he said, 'just as smooth
even without the fights.

I don't know how you do it.'
'When we stop worrying
about the bruises we all rise

in the darkness of our skins
and on the outside we appear
ominously smooth'

                      she told him. 'Look,
you don't keep even the
black and blue marks of my kisses.'

365 Days, One of them Circled

You swallowed the party,
blew out your candles, even put on
the shirt you didn't like
at first.

On the photos we look happy,
with no deeper meaning, and perhaps
this is the meaning.

The Circle

I have books
in which I take my walks.

I have a world of trees –
very alive – I watch them.

And the celestial bodies
circle around me

(with respect).
Every evening the moon

shows up
shedding light upon me.

Sometimes I am in a bad mood.
I am the perfect person –

wrapped all over in skin.
Thorough movements

are accomplished inside.
The circle of the universe

comes and goes out of my pores
babbling of eternity.

Singing: everything can be attained by change.
Eternity,

only accessible through change.
Perfection,

only accessible through change.
Eternity, perfection,

I sing the unattainable.
It is my turn to sing today.

Our Friends Come Back to Open Our Eyes

     Dear kitten,
I seem to know you, you are the soldier
who died for me in the Coliseum – the crowds roared
when they let out the tiger.
I didn't want any of you two to get hurt.
How did you run me down through time?
Was there really such a soldier?
Is transmigration possible?

     Anything is possible but quite unlikely,
perhaps as improbable as out of all 6 billion people today
you turn out to be Pasteur, Paracelsus or Pope Joan,
and the need for real heroes should not
exceed common sense.
Look, we are obvious, warm to each other,
but who can guarantee for the world?
Try to read better books,
     answered the kitten.

Visiting Hours

The noise during the visiting hours –

A! A! A! A! O! E! E! E! –

like in a public bath – the water washes away the consonants
and the dissonants bark under the low dome
pressed down by the heat.
The simple conversation falls apart
                              into interjections
crooked like the bodies around –
I almost forget it is a hospital –
today you are weak but not angry.

A leftover smile.
                You took a picture of me
before I turned the corner.

My Grandmother and I

To my grandmother and yours

'My grandmother and I got on with each other
without meaning to. I didn't mean
to say that.'

'I remember how she kneaded and kneaded
with her arthritic hands while I hung around
asking her to give me a little piece of dough.
Oh, get away from me, she would shoo me off.
This was her part.'

'Sometimes she joked
saying, I'll go visit the Toy Letter Box,
instead of, you know what, that was
her own joke. She had more of them.'

'At other times we sat at dusk on the balcony
and that was all I needed.'

'Once I told her
the scientists found there was no God.
She stood silent for a while and
then said, well, I think otherwise.
That is how the dispute between
my grandmother and all the world's scientists ended
and some days I think they were right
and some other days
I think she knew better.'

'Every morning my grandmother would pour
a drop of her coffee in my milk.
I imagined she was a space visitor
sent to Earth on a special mission
to take care of me
and I still dreaded the day
I would grow up,
but I felt better.'

Cat Exhibition

Persians with faces
like sand deposits,

Siamese females with eyes
like the sky over the emperor,

Angora toms, lazy and watchful
like harem eunuchs.

Name: Domingo
Breed: Cornish Rex

Father: Eldora's Playboy
Mother: Lucrecia

Children are happy to touch
their tails. Crowding up,

we worship
our own selection.

On my way home a cat comes out of
the dustbins and rubs against my legs.

Good evening, princess in exile,
how farest thou?

Omens

In those days my mouth
        developed an ulcer in the corner,
        a central heating pipe leaked,
        we got poisoned at dinner,
        and there were other portents too.
And then he told me that
        I was so arrogant in everything
        I seemed to do for us both.
            I.
            He!
        It's not true.
        It's not true,
I wanted to shout in a loud voice
        but my voice came out low
        and instead of fighting,
        its thin body
        walked away down the street.

A Plan

I'm going to buy strawberries,
then I'll drink tea,
but not before that.
I know one has to work
but I can't do it all the time,
and as for the books I haven't read,
I'll read them one by one.

Linda

(1976-1990)

Linda was not a human being
and burial was not obligatory.
In the cold January morning
my mother and I
walked round the yard,
she, with a small box in her hands,
I, with a knife,
scratching the earth here and there,
but I already knew
two feet was too deep a hole
for a kitchen knife
in the January morning.
In the box rattled Linda –
a small dog, her tongue
clenched between her teeth.
The eyes are conclusive.
She is cold to touch,
forever freed from the joy to see me.
Smells of tumor.
I cannot shake off the feeling
that upstairs at home
in a single unceasing moment
she is still waiting
for the iron coat of pain
to slacken.

The two-member funeral procession
headed for the garbage containers.

The Pigeon

The pigeon, clawless,
limps a little,
assesses a piece of bread quickly,
then pecks at it.
I know there are wood-pigeons too.
Perhaps they coo full-throatedly,
flitting like shiny symbols.
This pigeon here has grown up by the church,
many times he has eaten food to honour the departed
or posed with wedding guests for a picture,
and he reconnoitres every crescent-roll bag.
His round stare commands the situation,
as he limps up to the food.
It is a sad job,
a citizen's dignity.

Faith

Stefcho from Slatina Town
believes in Batman.
He believes in Baba Yaga too,
in Santa Claus, the fairies,
the aliens, Dracula,
the seven dwarfs and
Snow White.

At night he prays:
'Please, Batman,
kill Baba Yaga
who told Santa I
hated the fairies
who didn't help me
when I dreamed that
Dracula was an alien
who turned into a dwarf
to kidnap Snow White.
Snow White, please stay
away from Dracula,
but most of all: don't
get a crush on Batman.
He's a cut-throat killer, I tell you.

So We Shall Fly through Space

Radio amateurs on a desert island,
that's what we are, turning the buttons.
Bleeping sounds come out
and orbit the Earth
like a sputnik
or a meteor gone astray
from its flock.
Maybe a thousand years will pass
in this orbiting but what
             does it matter
if the people have already left
             or the receivers
have been replaced by higher technology?
What remains is
our joy from the bleeping.

What remains is what you
told me last night.

Your words were unforgettable
like bubbles in front of a face
under the water.

Anyway, by now
We can only breathe mouth-to-mouth.

Closed Figures

Everywhere nets of people
support each other
and allow no leaks.
The impulse runs
in closed figures
and although it looks good, it isn't.
Somebody told me in a dream:
'The puppets, loyal to their master,
get the worst of it.
Write that down.'
There, I wrote it.

A Summit Meeting

Raisa,
the Russian lady next door,
comes from Siberia.
'Yif you ask anothyer Russian,
they'll say 'from Lyeningraad',
they all from Lyeningraad,
but I say it as it is – from Sibeer,
from kolhoz.'
We sit with Raisa on a bear skin,
drinking herbal tea.
Presently the doorbell rings:
'Dobur den.' I hear a clear American accent
and two ginger Mormons, unaware of their
mission's impossibility,
beam in the doorway.
'We come in the name of the
Living Gaad, the living Gaad'
'Oy, Gospodi,
yeverybody knows Gord nyever died.'
'Do you believe in Gaad?'
'Buzz off, you idiot.'

Today, on the 16th floor,
the big ones met.

Dobur den (Добър ден) – 'good day' in Bulgarian.

Parting

From far away I could hear myself talking
while you were crying as if
an asteroid had blown the earth off
from under your feet.

Or:

From far away you could hear yourself talking
while I was crying as if
an asteroid had blown the earth off
from under my feet.

The Wedding of Life, Sleep and Death

'Life is a dream'.
(Calderon de la Barca)

If sleep is a brother of death,
then death, thus related,
becomes a cousin of life.
I fall asleep and offer space
for the cousins to meet.
I love family gatherings.
The musicians play wildly and
the wine stains don't stand out.
One day we all wake up in our beds
and feel ashamed we've done it
with each other.

Ivanka Wants to Kill Her Daughter

Ivanka wants to kill her daughter
but what stops her? Maybe
it's the daughter.
Every evening the crash of broken tableware
makes wrinkles in our neighbors' soup;
their shrieks string up four or five flats
and end up in the bedroom of the sixth.
Someone there doesn't know
how to keep on dreaming
and hates them.
We could add a thing or two.
Ivanka and her daughter treat themselves
with emotion-blunting pills.
Supposedly they take them.

Big deal.

First:
Sofia is a sum of dots
in ratio to the altitude of Mt. Fortune
Second:
They will never find happiness
with so much unattainable sincerity.

The Fear

What a big black butterfly,
no, no, just a geometric sparrow
moving without fluttering,
flying like nothing else,
but the way he does it -
a bat
in the stairwell?
Smaller
than a big olive, he clung
adroitly to the wall
in an asserted bat-posture,
head downwards,
trying hard to see where he is.
I wonder what happens
in his agglutinated eyes?
A sharp black piece
off the night's skin,
plainly frightened
by the light
he cannot see.
A familiar feeling.

The Harbour

The guide was wearing
a theatrical black cloak with the hood up.
He was showing us around the city but perhaps he was
its only landmark –
this city was stony and grey, like so many others,
and we rambled about its mundane streets.
Suddenly
our guide stopped:
'This'
he said, stretching out his arm to point

'is the harbour.'

And there it was, among the houses,
in the middle of the street –
an ocean started,
so blue it overflowed in the sky,
its waters breathing gently
by the tops of my shoes.
An enormous sigh was released
somewhere in the middle of the town;
it passed like wind through me
and whizzed into the horizon.

A-A-A-A-A-A-A-A-A-A-A-H

The blue absorbed it.

Only then I noticed
my guide had no eyebrows
and his skin was too tight, if he had
any skin at all.

I couldn't see the eyes
he watched me with.

I thought: "*Everything is so impressive, so grand, right in the middle of the grey city, in the narrow street, so beautiful and unexpected, so different –*

is it for me?"

(He was already gone.)

A few hours later I knew.
It hadn't been for me.

Free Fall

Let us jump together
hand in hand in the sky,
fly under its soft palate
and, reversing time,

fall behind its magnifying lens
back to beginners' slope,
awkward new as we were then
and enlarged by hope.

Passing by the City of Sort

Because we didn't buy lottery tickets,
we missed our chance to rule the world.
Our bus takes us away through the mountains
while we chew over the omission.
The ticket money is poisoning our pockets.

Maya: They said in a film that if you
don't buy a 200 euro dress,
you become richer by 200 euro.

I: In New York I took a look at the
Chrysler Building but it was a no deal.
Not at this price!

Maya: You've saved your money. They
tried to sell me the Louvre
but no, sir, I was not buying.

I: Why, I refused an offer for Taj Mahal
complete with North India. So what am I doing
with all this money now?

If you stop before buying the world,
you will be infinitely rich.

If you buy it, you become a beggar.

If you are like Maya and me on the bus
at least you have plans.

Sort – 'luck' in Catalan. There is a constant flow of people in the city who come with the purpose of buying lottery tickets.

The Truth Will Make You Free

To look for a new job.

The Conversationalist

He stooped over the grass
and it waved at him.
Then he went deeper
under some tall trees
talking to them in order to
take part in their endeavour.
The light shone
inside the air
and was expanding into a ball.
Then he met a bony man –
his face was lifeless
and his eyes busy –
who, without seeing him,
passed through his body.
That didn't disturb him.
Well, he thought, dead people still
haven't mastered our tongue, and he
went on whispering with the leaves.

The Winner

The winner scored a goal.
The winner loved
to score goals.

The crowd in the stadium shot up
like the blossom of a giant
sea anemone.

His teammates
trampled him with their kisses
and erased his features

touching him
for luck.
In the colossal singing cup

the enemy's goal keeper
still swayed on his knees.
The cameras were shooting him

just to show if there is life
at rock bottom.
Beyond the stadium there was silence.

Beyond beyond the stadium there was silence.
Beyond beyond beyond the stadium
there was silence too.

The Trace

Yesterday while I was
traveling in the tram
I saw on the pavement
a bright trace.
How could I forget
it was we who left it
a month ago – our hands
were full of presents
and we were joking
on our way back.

Advantage

The one-legged Gypsy
        was begging behind the wind at a February corner,
but people steered clear of him as if he was already blessed
        with more than he deserved;
after all,
        he shivered with one leg only.

St. Valentine is a Martyr of Ancient Rome

What made you bother to send me postcards
in the shape of a heart –
the cardiologists reject it.
The economists warned
that commercial holidays
        are bad for your health.
For the sake of the gullible
each sociologist holds a slice of pie chart
with rate of people expecting Santa
        secretly labeled 'blockheads'.
Do I remember? All right,
I do.

Eva

Somewhere upstairs
Eva sinks.
Among fountains of imaginary flowers –
no one brings her real ones
any more.
She fades. Her body
congeals.
She no longer talks.
In a small room under the stairs
the fashion magazines with her photos
shrivel up.
Her waters flow
in tubes now.
Her dismantled nerves allow
no more than a wink.
'How are you?' I climb invisible
between the vases full of sharp sword lilies.
(Daffodils crunch underfoot.)
Eva sits up in her bed and feels
for her slippers.
    Like you see,
she spreads two hands which in fact
she cannot move.
    It's time,
the props begin to crumble.

Asen

My friend Asen bought his
mother a fur coat for which
he spent every single lev
from his five-year salary
as a doctor. (She is a widow.
He is single.) It is a gesture
sadder than any poem and
that is why I say it
this way.

Feelings

Once again I see the creep with the moustache
shake his wife's rugs, glancing furtively around.
They seem to be a happy couple –
she bakes pies for him,
he shakes her rugs.
Every day I see them on their balcony,
sometimes him and sometimes her,
and I miss them during the holidays
I will miss them if I ever go away –
the house, the ivy, the rain drain pipe
unbuttoned in three places, and
the creep with the moustache.
I get addicted to the things I hate.

The Colonel's Widow

Minka, Colonel Gruyev's widow,
yesterday tells me:
He, my new comrade in life,

is very much into hygiene. Twice a week
we take a bath together and then
I throw the towels out to dry

in the sunshine.
I say: Minka, dear,
don't strain yourselves too hard!

Slow down!

The Bald Boy

The bald boy in his usual
baseball cap once again sits
in the bus by the window,
watching outside.
His billed cap, meant to shade the sun,
is like the mafia men sunglasses –
at night it hides nothing.
With this cap he looks
like a traffic lights pole,
stuck in amber.

Only the most fervent and cold-blooded will be saved.

As for him, he is already in hell –
neither too sad, nor too happy,
just accommodated.
His inner self,
poorly dressed in a hairless body,
has long ago stopped shivering
but has dropped the strings:
the face hangs
untaught
to smile back.

Reconstructing the Scene

In the street
a coat collar
marked the spot
where the woman with
the shopping bags
melted
while praying for a miracle to happen.

A Few Extra Chromosomes

The eyes on his big head look as if
taken from a smaller creature,
a Capuchin monkey, perhaps. Mum and Dad
love him very much and take care of him –

he is happy about his new tattoo.
A real man's thing. A football emblem,
probably dad's football team. He shows it.
Joyfully he hides from the sun's rays

into the swimming pool, and when they
find him there, he smiles at them.
Look, it's good for swimming. Good
for swimming – he repeats politely

to anyone who would care to know.
Mum and Dad grow older with each day
but they don't look it. He is no longer a boy either
but that is difficult to grasp too.

Then we queued for lunch, holding our trays.
'I know what I like' he announced
and took only meatballs.
At least one of us knew.

Tibet

The whole road is besprinkled with lanterns,
the lamas are smiling. They banter each other;
gathered around the cold fire,
they smear it with fingers over their bodies,
licking the flames.
My distant shadows, it has been long since
I started to crawl towards you
in pieces. Somebody has to skin the fatigue,
frighten the habit.
I know I too am a free person,
but I forget.

Sometimes it is Not Important Who Sings

During the concert, between
Iron Men and Bark at the Moon
the music kicked out at faces
of screaming kids,
rock veterans with thinning muscles
bashed their gray ponytails, teenage girls

riding on the shoulders of their jumping boyfriends
waved overheated lighters.
The stadium sang, sounding like an attempt
to run down the Hubble Telescope with the chorus,
and then Tanya, beer in hand, observed
that summer is good in itself,

and today it's even breezy. She
repeated it three times, shouting.
Up in the sky an airplane
was passing over us. I wished
I were in it, sitting by the window.
I was flying over the stadium, I saw

the violet spotlights, I could even see
myself on the steps with my beer half-empty,
and I told myself I would really like
to be in my place.
This picture
had no sound.

The Garden of Exquisite Silence

The white statues arch their necks,
keeping their empty marble gazes
bolted.
It is closed,
this door to the sculptor's hand
when the stone still
scraped the dust off its face.
Behind each statue's forehead
there is a message.
If you look for an answer,
you break the head.
If you keep the head safe,
you do not get anywhere.
If you break the head,
you may still not get an answer.
Decide faster.

In the Third Quarter

All slim bohemians
wind up as paunchy simians.
The red veins have
a hard time keeping
the eyes in the sockets.
The nose is big, pudgy,
a pillow to sleep
your journey away. The chest
refuses to hear its own whistling
on your way upstairs.
The others can hear it.
And the loose skin over the elbows
stirs memories
like the empty mailbox of lovers
who ended in marriage.
In the morning
you shave somebody else's face.
In the morning
you shave somebody else's legs.
In the morning
you shave your own
promises grown
weed-thick.
Bohemianism
hates itself.

And a Key is No Longer Necessary

They drop like acrobats on ropes
from the sky, the years, and
it is all so dangerous –
a smashing circus show. Sometimes
you find yourself, sometimes you
get lost in the distance,
me peeling skin after bone.

> A dream is
> a captured castle – you capture it
> and remain inside.
>
> Poetry is
> a wall surmounted – you surmount it
> and remain inside.

Inside, inside.
Inside you hear everything,
but you don't make sense of it.

A Premonition of a Dream

I had died in my sleep.
I had died in my 28th year.

I saw many unfamiliar faces
of working, too busy people –
I was senseless of cold or hunger,
and to them I was stark invisible.

So short it was, thought I.
My 28 years now seem
to have never been here at all;
what a stupid no-time for anything.

So what I remember is gone,
and what I intended is meaningless,
and the faces around me are alien,
and those that I know – how'll they see me?

From the lifeless chasm of time
I cannot now but see
the minutes that burst in the dense world
as they fleetingly pass through me.

The Refuge

When you look up and see
how the water laps in the well,
how the wise men have leaned
above the edge, sipping from ladles,
how they lay claims against all
who ask them what day it is, how
they won't let the woman with the earthen jar
come close because she is web-toed,
how they line the desert people up
according to beard length
and still don't let them drink,
you start thinking about yourself

without thinking about yourself.
Underground water travels
all the way down to the earth's heart
along silver capillaries.

Each day is inevitably different.

Washed out by the flow,
drowned by the darkness,
perhaps you pack a little luggage
for a few days to come,
oh, geographic monster
with coral-grown teeth.

Put out these dots in your eyes.
If we are to die together
it doesn't have to be now.

At the End of the Summer

How could I leave my children alone by the
swimming pool? They have jumped from the top board

and are still alive. Now they enter the sea.
Can they swim? I thought I already had

a life of my own, but my ears are in their lungs
and my eyes are inside theirs. Somewhere

far away I drown and fight to keep afloat,
but I am not with them, and cannot be there, and

swept ashore at this safe land I am
sinking elsewhere.

The Breeder

She came in with a piece of fresh meat.

In the room
the young unfledged eagle
already had
tough legs,
beak,
feathers,
and some old fuzz trapped
in their scissors.
'Look at you,'
said the woman. 'And I worried
whether you'll live.'
His new eye
stared at her
and recognised no one.

An Epic

a life like in a dream
a life like in a film
a life like a projection
on a screen – where are
the images? where do
all kisses after those plane crashes
and then the credits with the actors
and the heroes disappear to?
where are you heroes going?
what is to happen with your names?
only the white screen remains
comparatively white and
patched up in the corner.

the auditorium is cool and large

the auditorium is shadowy and deep
unlike the credits

I do not want to leave

The Awakening

After he had been successively
pressured by his boss, broken down by work,
stabbed in the back by colleagues, trapped by
circumstances and crushed by responsibilities,

peace finally came.
The pills in his right pocket
stopped shrinking in number.
Music

was no longer a nuisance.
In fact, it poured in through
all sensory channels
gathering inside him

in a festive vortex.
It was difficult to explain
how, after so many deaths, he
wound up here, in this bubble of

sunlight,
moving around with him.
No glowing words hovered here,
words he could arrange in a

reportage from the place of events.
There were no events either –
the cut didn't bleed.
High above the world he dangled his feet

off the edge of his transparent garden,
watching himself.
Below, among the busy traffic a man
was crossing the street with a smile.

The Game

We were playing cards with God
when he trumped my king with a two.
'But God, according to the rules
you cannot do this' I brandished
my fan of cards.
'Then think up of some
explanation' he said.
And dealt again.